BUNKY:

MY LIFE AS A KID

Other books by
Dennis Perry

Young Adult-Fiction
Yakabou Must Choose

Children's Books-Fiction
Sunny vs. the Dragon
Achoo!

Adult Books-Fiction
The Copper Thieves
Mad Dog Steel Time
Missing in Paradise

Adult Books-Non-Fiction
Bunky
Don't Run Over a Snake's Tail, Slowly

BUNKY:
MY LIFE AS A KID

DENNIS PERRY

iUniverse, Inc.
Bloomington

BUNKY, MY LIFE AS A KID

iUniverse books may be ordered through booksellers or by contacting:

iUniverse
1663 Liberty Drive
Bloomington, IN 47403
www.iuniverse.com
1-800-Authors (1-800-288-4677)

ISBN: 978-1-4759-4302-3 (sc)
ISBN: 978-1-4759-4303-0 (ebk)

Printed in the United States of America

iUniverse rev. date: 08/08/2012

Dedication

For Del and Camille Backus

Foreword

The stories in *Bunky* are true stories from my childhood, as I remember them.

Like the original Grimm Brothers tales, some readers may think they aren't suitable for children.

Bunky and the 'Gypsies'

My mother was a single mom in 1943. For the first years of my life I lived with her in my Grandparents' small home in Glenns Ferry, Idaho. Their home was always a busy place with the comings and goings of my mom's two sisters and four brothers, plus all of my cousins.

The limitations of my immediate world, as a child, included a medium sized grassy yard enclosed by tall lilac bushes and a white picket fence in front of the house separating it from the street. My instructions were simple-don't go out of the yard or into the street.

In Bunky and the 'Gypsies' I violated the instructions I knew very well.

The small carnival set up its booths and tents down the street from my grandparents' house. The carnival folk passed through Glenns Ferry every summer on their way to Boise, Idaho. Along the way they stopped off in all the small towns. Mountain Home, an Air Force town was the next stop after Glenns Ferry. Then the brightly painted trucks and trailers with their cargoes of rides and games would set up for a couple of weeks in Boise.

The carnival people lived in their trucks and trailers while they worked the local towns with dime pitches, baseball tosses, a Ferris wheel, carousal, and other assorted rides.

During the day the carnival was all sound. The pitch men shouting at the towns people as they passed by.

"Hey, hey throw a ball today! You can play! You can win!"

"Buy your girl some cotton candy!"

"Win your girlfriend a teddy bear!"

"No one goes away empty handed!"

The small empty lot they had set up in was dusty from trampling feet as the summer sun beat down. Kids drank RC's and Root Beer, and adults drank draft beer from a tent at the back of the lot.

At noon I followed my grandparents to the carnival. My mother worked at a local café until late evening. At five years old it was my first time at the carnival and I was taking everything in with wide-opened green eyes. The dark brown skinned men and women standing beside the games and rides especially interested me.

"Hey there Sonny," they called to me as I passed by their attractions."

"Take a ride," the Ferris wheel man offered and then looked at Grandpa Backus who would have to pay the $.25 fee.

"Can I go on the Ferris wheel?" I pleaded with my grandfather.

"Sure, if it's okay with your grandmother, it's okay with me," he said and dug into his pocket for a quarter.

Neither of my grandparents wanted to go on the ride so they let me get into the Ferris wheel bucket seat by myself. A carnival man, wearing a baseball cap, helped me into the seat and fastened the safety belt around my waist. *The man smelled of cigarettes and beer like grandfather did after he came back from a walk downtown*, I thought as I settled back into the seat.

The carnival man smiled at me in a friendly way and whispered that he would stop the ride at the top so I could look out over the town.

I grabbed the bar in front of me and gave the man a faint smile. The man pushed the Ferris wheel control handle slowly forwards and the Ferris wheel turned, creaking and rattling in its metal frame. I looked down at my grandparents when the bucket seats tipped down a little and then started upward again. At the top of the ride the man in the baseball cap pulled the handle backwards and the Ferris wheel rocked back and forth and then stopped.

Setting in the Ferris wheel seat at the top of the ride there was nothing between me and the open sky. I could see the town's water tower over my shoulder and the winding Snake River on my left side. It was very exciting to look down and see all the people walking the dusty midway between the carnival attractions. Grandma Backus waved at me when I looked her way and I waved back.

The Ferris wheel man pushed the handle again and the Ferris wheel started down toward the ground. After a couple times around the wheel finally stopped. I jumped onto the loading step and hugged my grandmother and held my grandfather's hand.

We continued walking through the carnival. Everyone spoke to me, asking me if I wanted to throw dimes in a dish, or did I want to toss a baseball at the stuffed cats. Of course I wanted to do all of those things, and grandpa kept reaching into his pocket for more dimes.

When it was time for us to leave the carnival I had eaten hot dogs, pink cotton candy, and popcorn. I'd drunk soda pop and eaten ice-cream. I remember really liking the carnival and all of the men and women at the carnival that I'd heard the townspeople calling 'Gypsies'.

Back at my grandparents' house, Shorty, my grandparents' pet terrier, ran to meet me, wagging his stumpy tail. I shared my cotton candy with Shorty and patted his head while Shorty licked my sun-burned cheeks.

My grandparents had settled in to listen to the radio, so I went outside to play in the green yard surrounded by lilac bushes. I wasn't supposed to go out of the yard but I really wanted to go talk to the 'Gypsies' at the carnival.

Later when it was time for me to come in from the lawn, my grandparents called me, but Shorty ran up to the front porch alone, wagging his tail. It seemed like only Shorty had followed the rules about not leaving the yard.

Although Glenns Ferry was a small town there were dangerous things that could happen to a five year old boy who wandered away from home.

Grandma Backus spoke to the next door neighbors, the Clarks, who were cousins and asked them to help look for their five year old cousin. The Clarks had older children of their own who were instructed to help search for me.

The adults and children of both families spread out to cover the neighborhood. The kids soon became tired of searching and used the search as an excuse to go to the carnival. So it shouldn't be a surprise that they were the first ones to find me and send their fastest runner to find the adults and tell them they had found Bunky.

Margie, my mother, home from work, and Grandma Backus followed the young Clark offspring to the headquarters trailer of the carnival where the carnival manager was talking to the group of children standing around me.

I ran to hug my mother as soon as I saw her. Then I asked her very seriously if I could join the carnival.

"The 'Gypsies' were all nice to me," I explained, without meaning them any insult.

"They showed me how to be an elephant," and I grabbed my nose with my left hand and put my right arm through the crook of my left arm and waved it up and down slowly just like an elephant would do.

"They said they would teach me how to talk to people when they come to the carnival. And the people who come to the carnival are all rubes who just want to give their money away, and if they don't want to give it away then they are cheap bastards."

The carnival manager shrugged his shoulders and gave the adults a lop-sided grin like what he had said was all a joke.

Margie and Grandma Backus looked kind've shocked when they heard me use the swear word; and they were also suspicious that the 'Gypsies' were going to kidnap me until they found out the carnival manager had already called the sheriff who had stopped at their house and talked to Grandpa Backus while they had all been out searching.

Epilogue

During the next two weeks I was happy to entertain everyone with my adventures about when I was with the 'Gypsies'. At the end of the two weeks a sad thing happened. Shorty, the little terrier that was like a family member violated the rule he had followed when I hadn't the night when I ran away to the carnival. Shorty went into the street and a passing car turned the corner and ran over the beloved family pet. Shorty was laid to rest under the lilac bushes with tears from me, and the words, "He was a good little dog.'

Bunky and
the Big Parade

Before entering this July 4th costume contest I have clear memories of dressing up as a cowboy in my grandparents' house with the help of my cousins and my Uncle Donny. I may have wanted to go to the parade, but I don't think it was my idea to enter the contest.

Also, after turning eleven or twelve years old no one, relatives or otherwise could have forced me to wear cowboy clothes. Cowboy clothes were, and still are definitely part of Idaho culture, but for some reason I can't explain I never embraced cowboy culture.

It was the Fourth of July in the small Idaho railroad town called Glenns Ferry. It was a railroad town because the Union Pacific Railroad had trains running through the town with a passenger stop and a crew change over there. The railroad contributed to making Glenns Ferry a prosperous small town. It's true that highway 30, at that time, a major transportation route, provided daily travelers at the local cafes and bars. The permanent residents of Glenns Ferry numbered about 2,000 back then. The population is down to 1,030 now because the new interstate highway has taken away all but the most desperate travelers, and the railroad doesn't run passenger trains anymore.

Back in 1949, Glenns Ferry was still a growing town that got up a celebration on the Fourth of July. There would be a parade, a picnic, and fireworks in the evening. All of the surrounding farm families benefited from the railroad and the highway. They shopped at the grocery store and the department store, they took loans out at the local bank, and they filled prescriptions at the town's only drug store. They also came to town for the Fourth of July parade.

At the shotgun shack where I was spending the summer with my grandparents everyone was excited, and I was excited like only a six year old can be.

Even though the shotgun shack, so called because if a shotgun is aimed in the front door and the trigger is pulled a full pattern of pellets will go through the shack and exit through the back door, wasn't fancy, it was my home for the summer.

The small house had only one real bedroom. To the side of the rear hallway entrance an indoor toilet with a large white porcelain bathtub on ball and claw feet had been added.

In this small house it seemed as though no matter how many relatives showed up there was always room for everyone to have a place to sleep and sit at the white enameled metal kitchen table, even if they had to do it in shifts.

Today was exciting because I had permission to wear a cowboy outfit put together from clothes borrowed from my uncles and cousins. I had a large cowboy hat and a red bandana to complete the outfit. In reality I generally didn't like to wear cowboy clothes; especially cowboy boots since I had wide feet and cowboy boots always pinched my toes. I would rather wear black and white sneakers. After a week or so the sneakers would stretch out and become very comfortable.

"Let's see what you look like," my older cousin Diana said. She looked at the Levis and the too large red and black checkered shirt tucked into my blue jeans. She adjusted the red bandana so the knot set to one side and the ends flared out jauntily. When she was satisfied she picked up the white cowboy hat that was about two sizes too big and set it just over my forehead, and settled it so I could see from underneath it.

"Boy, do you ever look like Roy Rogers or Gene Autry", she exclaimed.

"Gene Autry," I blurted out, "he's my favorite."

"Donny, come in here," Diana yelled from the living room to the back room where he was reading. (Donny was my mother's brother.) "You've got to see Bunky. He's going to win first prize at the parade today."

Donny came into the living room. At twenty years old he was a handsome young man. He had short brown hair and his soft brown eyes were filled with curiosity for all things mechanical and for all things in the natural world around him. He stood six foot tall and I admired him very much.

"You know what, I think you're right," he agreed. "But he still needs something to get the whole picture right, Hold on just a minute and I'll be right back," he said. He left the living room and went into the kitchen to search through the many kitchen drawers that served as a kind of cabinet of curiosities for past treasures collected by all of my uncles.

Diana and I heard Donny rustling through many drawers and then he was back in the living room with one hand behind his back.

"What do you suppose I have here?" he teased me.

"Spurs," I guessed. I was no stranger to cowboy paraphernalia, although I actually preferred Flash Gordon to all of the cowboys.

"No, guess again."

"Stop teasing him," Diana said.

"Okay. Here you go," Uncle Donny said and pulled a rusty old western style pistol out from behind his back. It was a large caliber pistol used by the pioneers who had crossed Idaho on their way to Oregon generations earlier. There was no chance the pistol would ever fire again. Its barrel was filled with rust and the trigger was frozen in place. But, from a distance it still would look dangerous tucked into the belt of a six year old.

Everyone thought my costume was great. The parade would be in two hours. I strutted through the house with my hand on the butt of the rusted pistol.

My Grandpa Backus returned from an errand and so he and Uncle Donny left the white painted shotgun shack with me. A resident of Glenns Ferry can get from almost anywhere to anywhere else with a four or five block walk. We were going from the wrong side of the railroad tracks to Main Street where the parade would start. All the costumed contestants would enter their names on a list at a table in front of the bank. Then the parade would go down Main Street and end up in front of the Orpheum Theater.

Donny helped me sign up for the costume contest. The Glenns Ferry boosters' club, called the Pilots was running the contest and would be awarding a $50.00 prize for the best costume.

Jim Allen, the president of the Pilots took my information and I was entered in the contest. My white cowboy hat had just barely poked up over the edge of the table.

"Say, Donny you know there's a fifty cent entry fee for this young cowboy. Are you paying it?" asked Jim Allen.

"Here's your fifty cents Jim," Donny said as he handed the man in the orange and black jacket with a black ship's helm on it, a silver fifty cent piece with liberty on one side and an eagle on the other side.

"It looks like you've got more than fifty dollars there. What are you going to do with the extra?"

"Well, you know we always pay for the hot dogs and sodas at the park on the 4th. It generally comes out that we have to kick in ten or twenty dollars out of our budget. Are you worried everything isn't on the up and up?"

Donny and Jim had played together as cousins and Donny knew Jim to be a "little sharp" as the expression goes.

"No Jim, I'm not worried," Donny smiled as he gave me my entry number.

I lined up with the other contestants behind a real horse drawn stagecoach on loan from the local historical society. It was painted black and had red leather upholstery. Ruby Jenson, dressed in her homecoming gown, road atop the stagecoach with the stagecoach driver. She carried a dozen red roses donated by Ronnie's flower shop. Ruby, a nice girl, waved and smiled at the townspeople lining the sidewalks as the sorrel horses pulled the stagecoach slowly down Main Street.

The sidewalk crowd was made up of people who weren't in costume; and who had come to the parade to see family members or neighbors in costumes as they marched behind the stagecoach.

A few veterans carrying Old Glory marched directly behind the stagecoach. As they passed the crowd women and children put their hands over their hearts and men who had been in the service saluted.

Among the costumed marchers there were Chinese coolies, not real coolies of course, although Idaho had plenty of Chinese left over from the gold rush days whose descendants had later become citizens. There were Huck Finns and Tom Sawyers in the parade along with flappers and children wearing their fathers' railroad clothes-red bandanas and stripped cotton cloth hats.

Behind all the costumed marchers came the Glenns Ferry Pilots in their orange and black silk jackets with a black ship's helm on the back ambling along waving at friends and family as they passed the crowded sidewalks.

Amid all of the costumed characters in the parade, the stagecoach driver dressed in western clothes from a time period seventy-five years earlier, had spotted me in my too large white cowboy hat, red scarf, with the huge real life revolver tucked into my trousers. He stopped the coach and talked briefly with a spectator on the sidewalk. He gestured back at me, and his friend the spectator, walked back to me and asked if my parents were around. I pointed at Uncle Donny and Grandpa Backus.

The spectator explained to them, "The stagecoach driver wants your boy on the seat beside him. Do you think that would be okay?"

"Bunky, do you want to ride on the stagecoach?" Grandpa Backus asked me.

I nodded yes.

Grandpa Backus answered the stagecoach drivers' friend, "Bunky says he'll do it."

The spectator picked me up and handed me off to the stagecoach driver. The driver made me comfortable on the seat beside him.

I was having a great time looking around and saw Ruby waving at everyone so I waved at everyone too. The driver took his hat off and waved it at friends, and so I took my big white cowboy hat off and waved it at the crowded sidewalk.

Donny and Grandpa Backus followed the stagecoach trying to get through the crowds on the sidewalks, but the stagecoach slowly pulled ahead of them until they could barely see me sitting with the driver.

It was a wonderful day. The sky was blue with no clouds in sight. Hot air radiated in waves from the sidewalks, the street and the brick buildings lining Main Street. I could see children licking pop cycles and drinking ice cold sodas. People were laughing and cheering and the sound echoed between the town buildings and the grassy banked railroad siding.

The judges' table was in front of the five lane bowling alley. The Mayor, Jim Allen, president of the Pilots, the chairwoman of the Pilots Women's Auxiliary, and the Commander of American Legend Post 32 were the judges.

As the costumed contestants marched by the judges' table each of the judges wrote down certain numbers displayed on the backs of the contestants. They had listened carefully as the crowd cheered one contestant or another. A lot of people in the crowd were laughing and pointing at me, the young cowboy seated beside the stagecoach driver. When they laughed and pointed I would lift my hat and wave at them. I put on a good show for a six year old.

The Mayor looked at me with the big gun tucked in my trousers and wrote a number on his pad. The chairwoman of the Women's Auxiliary laughed when I tipped my hat at her and she wrote a number on her pad. The Commander of the American Legion shifted his eyes away from the homecoming queen and after looking at the Mayor's pad he wrote the same number on his pad.

A young railroader and a girl dressed in a frilly pink dress like Becky Thatcher also made the judges' lists.

Contestants and relatives and friends from the crowd mingled happily at the end of the parade in front of the Orpheum Theater.

The Mayor, with Jim Allen standing by to help him award the prizes announced the winners for the costumed event. "The third place winner is . . ." and he paused for a moment for a dramatic effect, "number 37, the little railroader." The crowd clapped and cheered when Jim Allen handed a third place ribbon to the boy in the railroad engineer outfit. The Mayor went on, "The second place winner is number 22, the young lady dressed up as Becky Thatcher." The girl in the pink dress with a bow in her hair came forward to collect the second place prize and her ribbon. There was again clapping and cheering as she accepted her award.

Next the Mayor started to announce the first place winner. He paused for the dramatic moment again. "The first place winner is . . . number 48 the little cowboy in the big white hat."

The crowd cheered as Jim Allen helped me down from the stagecoach seat and pinned the first place ribbon on my shirt. While the crowd cheered Jim led me inside the stagecoach cabin.

Once Jim and I were inside the cabin out of view of the crowd Jim said, "You know Bunky," began the man in the orange booster jacket, "fifty dollars is an awful lot of money for you to carry around don't you think."

I pushed the cowboy hat back on my head and looked the man in the eyes, like only a six year old can do.

"I can give you a free ticket to the movies, plus fifty cents for popcorn and candy. That would be just about right wouldn't it?" He kept talking to me like I didn't have much choose in the matter.

"Well, that settles it I guess. You have your first place ribbon, a ticket to the movies and the fifty cents for the popcorn and candy. That's a good deal isn't it?" The big man finished his monologue while I stared at the movie ticket and the fifty cents he had just handed to me.

The president of the Pilots open the door of the stagecoach so the crowd could see me with the first place ribbon pinned to my red and black checkered shirt. When I climbed down the steps and jumped to the street the crowd cheered.

When I jumped off the bottom step of the coach, Jim Allen ducked around the side of the stagecoach and made his way back to the judges' table.

In a few minutes Uncle Donny and Grandpa Backus found me and asked what had happened at the award ceremony.

"I won first prize," I told them proudly. "And Mr. Allen gave me a movie ticket and fifty cents to buy candy with at the movie," I said holding up the movie ticket and the fifty cent piece.

"Is that all he gave you," Uncle Donny asked in a low tone of voice.

"Well, I got the ribbon too," I said, and pointed at the ribbon pinned to my shirt. It was indeed a fine blue ribbon in the tradition of State Fairs and Four H ribbons.

"And that, with the ticket and the fifty cent piece was all that he gave you?" Uncle Donny asked again in an even lower tone of voice.

"That's all," I answered.

"Well, well," Uncle Donny said. "Maybe I'd better go talk to Mr. Jim Allen."

Uncle Donny was generally a mild mannered man, but you could tell when he spoke in the low tone of voice he wasn't the person you would want angry at you.

Donny found Jim by the beer tent. He was sipping on an Olympia beer.

"Hey Jim," Donny began speaking to his cousin. "I just talked to Bunky. He looked real good with the blue ribbon pinned to his checkered cowboy shirt. I guess all the judges thought he looked good enough to win that fifty dollar prize, huh?"

"Oh, I wanted to talk to you about that," Jim replied, sheep faced with a little beer foam hanging on his chin where he had jerked his hand in surprise after hearing about the fifty dollars. "I kind of told Bunky I'd hang on to the fifty dollars for him. But I'll let you hold on to it if you think that's better."

"You know exactly what I think Jim." Donny said with an edge to his voice. "I'll take that fifty dollars and give it to Bunky's mom and she can look after it."

"Sure, sure, I got the fifty, right here in my pocket," Jim told Donny as he dug into his jeans pocket to find the folded twenties and a ten and hand them over.

Epilogue

I used the movie ticket at the Orpheum Theater. I also bought popcorn candy, and soda with the fifty cent piece.

My mom put the fifty dollar prize away. She would use it to buy school clothes and school supplies when I started school in the fall.

On top of winning the fifty dollars I had a big surprise coming. Mom married my stepfather and we moved to a new home with new cousins and uncles and aunts. But, for the time being, until the summer was over I sat happily watching a movie and eating popcorn.

Bunky at the Circus

When I was five years old mom met, and married Everett Perry. Soon after the marriage mom and I moved, with Everett, to Nampa, Idaho. We lived there with Grandfather Perry and Everett's two brothers and their wives.

From this time forward, as a youngster, I would spend summers living with my Backus grandparents. During these visits I had several adventures with Backus cousins. Bunky at the Circus *was one of those adventures.*

Cousin Butch, in the story, was one of the many cousins who also visited or stayed at the Backus home.

Although Butch and I resembled characters in the 50's movie Stand By Me, *in which the older boys bullied the younger boys, Butch was my protector.*

In the summer of 1949 I was spending summer vacation with my Grandparents. I was born in Glenns Ferry, Idaho in 1943. I was born a city boy, if a small town of 2,000 souls could be called a city. I'd left younger brother Carl at home with my parents and now I'd be on my own, staying with my grandparents.

Living on a farm near Nampa, Idaho had its own excitements, but Circus posters weren't one of them.

Now, at the start of my vacation I watched as a deeply tanned man brushed paste on the back of a brightly colored poster and then slapped it against a bare wall between buildings on Main Street.

The circus poster in red, yellow, and orange screamed like a side show barker-*The circus is coming to town!* The Advance Man, if he could be granted such an exalted title, plastered the posters where ever he could find a bare wall in the small railroad town of Glenns Ferry.

Glenns Ferry as its name implied had grown beside Gustavus Glenn's commercial ferry that began taking pioneers across the Snake River in 1863. The ferry service had been replaced by a sturdy local bridge when the railroad came through.

Glenns Ferry wasn't large enough to rate a full sized three ring circus, but once a year a smaller circus arrived by rail. Although small it had all the wild animals, lions, tigers, monkeys, and tame elephants advertised on the posters.

As it set loaded on the railroad flat cars the circus wasn't yet a circus. The large rolls of brown canvas, tall wooden poles and stacks of wide planks had to be unloaded and assembled. Circus roustabouts would supervise the setting up of tents, laying down a performers' ring, and the erection of bleachers for the audience. For economic and probably publicity reasons the circus owners made a rule that the assembling of the tents and bleachers would be done by the local boys and young men, who then receive free tickets to one evening show.

This was smart because they would want to bring their sweethearts or brothers and sisters and would buy more tickets.

Before the show could start everything had to be unloaded from the railroad siding into a weedy dry field. Soon, trampled by the comings and goings of boys and men dragging poles and canvas, a dust cloud rose over the field.

An elephant, directed by its handler, pulled a large center pole erect with an even plodding effort.

Every boy in Glenns Ferry wanted a ticket to the circus, so there were plenty of volunteers to help the roustabouts unfold and erect the tent, build the center performers' ring, and then assemble the audience bleachers.

One of the teenagers named Butch was babysitting his younger cousin, which was yours truly. Butch told me, "One of these days you'll be big enough to do this stuff on your own. Right now you just stick with me, okay?"

Butch had crew cut blond hair. He wore Levis and a white shirt with a collar. He had penny loafers with a dime in both shoes. Butch was sixteen years old and he lived in Boise. He was a real big city teenager. I was six years old and wore a stripped T-shirt with blue jeans. For shoes I wore black Kids tennis shoes; my hair was brown, eyes green, and I was deeply tanned from working and playing outdoors on my parents' farm in Nampa, Idaho.

Even though the work was hard Butch and I did as we were told-dragging and pulling poles and the heavy tent canvas until the large circus tent rose from the dusty ground to provide an enclosed area for the show to come.

Next, a hardened roustabout yelled at several boys to begin putting together a metal frame work for the ring side bleachers.

The air soon filled with dust and weed pollen in the closed tent area. The dust settled on sweat covered faces and arms. The pollen caused those who were allergic to scratch and rub at their sweaty eyes.

Butch and I carried heavy planks to the metal frames. I was sweating just like Butch, but I smiled when I thought of the ticket I was earning.

"I'll get a ticket, won't I Butch," I questioned Butch? Butch smiled and nodded his head.

One of the roustabouts with a mean look to him saw Butch and I working together and smiled an evil smile. He came up to Butch and put his face into Butch's face.

"You can carry those planks yourself and I'm taking that boy to help me unload planks from the railroad car."

When Butch gave the man a questioning look, he said, "If you two want tickets you have to do as I say," he challenged Butch.

Butch gave him a bad look and didn't back up. He replied, "Those planks are too heavy for just one person and my cousin is working as hard as I am, so leave us alone."

The roustabout glared at Butch and raised his closed fist at him before he turned and walked away.

"Butch, are we going to get tickets," I asked again.

"Yah, we better get tickets or I'll find out why not. Come on let's finish unloading these planks for the bleachers like the first man told us to do."

The day was hot and the dusty, dry weeds beside the railroad tracks and in the field were quickly trampled flat. Grasshoppers jumped and flashed their wings taking flight with a whirring noise to get out of the way of the workers.

The roustabouts who were directing the setting up of the tents also ran the side shows, carnival games, and fast food stands that accompanied the circus that attracted the people from the town and made most of the money.

The small circus with its side shows was soon completed with the help of the town volunteers. The boys and men who had helped set up the tents stood in line in front of a circus trailer waiting for their free tickets.

A long line of young men and boys were waiting to get their tickets. Some of them smoked and joked around while they waited. Every one was sweaty and covered with fine white dust from the formerly vacant field.

Butch and I were standing with the others in front of the folding table where the tickets were being handed out.

The roustabout with an evil smile was one of the men handing out tickets. He took a look at Butch and said, "Only one ticket here. That kid;" and he pointed at me, "he didn't do enough work to earn a ticket."

Butch came from a family of four brothers and three sisters and he knew the value of the saying, *"A good offense is the best defense."*

"Suit your self," Butch said with an equally menacing smile on his lips. "But you should know that I have three older brothers and they all have friends, and if I have to come back with them it won't be to buy extra tickets. This town is a small place. We can find you easy enough," he said with his arms stiff and pressing down on his side of the table. "On the other hand, our whole family will want to come to the circus some time during the next three days. What do you think would be the smart thing to do? Give us two free tickets, or we'll come back like I promised."

The roustabout knew Butch wasn't kidding around. These small town rubes had a way of protecting their turf, and they didn't forget or forgive easily if they were pushed.

The other young men in line who had heard the conversation stopped their joking around and didn't appear to be taking too kindly to the roustabout's threats.

"Okay kid. You get your tickets," he said, shrugging his shoulders as if the whole thing hadn't happened.

As we walked away from the table I wanted to know why the man behind the table didn't want to give us the two tickets.

"You are going to run into jerks like him all the time. They think it's fun to give people a hard time because they have a little bit of authority. The ones like him will generally give in unless they have a couple of buddies backing them up. They don't expect whoever they are picking on to stand up to them. But you have to be careful when somebody with real authority, like a sheriff or a state trooper decides to get nasty, when that happens you had better start out and finish with a lot of, 'Yes sirs,' and 'No sirs,' and hope they don't decide to really get mean with you."

"Anyway," Butch said looking at the blue sky filled with plenty of sunshine, "we got the tickets. Let's go home and get cleaned up so we can go to the circus tonight."

Bunky and the Golden Prize

The Golden Prize *is written almost exactly as it happened. The story is a good story despite the troubled relationship between me and my stepfather.*

Every young person has an occasion involving conflict with a parent. Many adults reflect on these occasions in their childhood as character building events and excuse whatever punishment received as deserved.

I have to wonder if the adults involved in such interactions are acting out of strictly character building motives, or out of anger and frustration.

In my adult life as a teacher and as a professional librarian dealing with the public on a day to day basis, I've experienced both the desire to be rational, offering a truly adult perspective; and, unfortunately, also responding to youthful attitudes out of anger and frustration. In the end I know I've always regretted reacting with anger and frustration.

A small, southern Idaho dairy farm, set nestled under blue skies. I was an eleven-year-old boy living on the farm under these blue skies. I was kept and fed by my stepfather, who expected a great deal from me. There were chores to be done, and to be done competently.

On this particular summer day an older female, city cousin, named Kathy, had come to experience country life, and consequently also to be under my stepfather's care and authority.

We were sent by my stepfather to fetch a small herd of gentle dairy cows, grazing in deep waving, green grass, from hilly pastures into a dusty corral beside the milk barn, where they would also serve my stepfather, and our family by giving up their daily quota of milk.

Like Jack and Jill, Kathy and I walked a dusty farm lane from the corral to the grassy hill pastures. A shallow clear stream trickled along beside the dusty path.

Tall for her age, the dark haired girl looked toward the pasture and the cows. I was a little younger and shorter than my city cousin, and had done this chore hundreds, if not thousands of times, so I let my attention wonder, looking around under the blue sky.

The air was filled with the sweet smell of alfalfa and clover coming from the hay field next to the lane. With my eyes and ears I followed the yellow and black meadow larks and black birds hopping from fence post to fence post lining both sides of the farm lane. I listened to the birds singing, and inspected the clear stream beside the lane.

"Hey," I exclaimed excitedly to Kathy, "look at the goldfish there in the stream," I said.

Because I had fetched cows morning and night since I was six years old, this new event . . . I had never seen a fish in the trickling stream, let alone a gold fish with whiskers. It's a catfish; I thought searching my mind rooms and little used mind corners for likely comparisons to the shining creature swimming in the stream before me which had completely captured my attention.

As for my cousin, who was from the city, everything in the country was equally new to her. Fetching black and white Holstein and mellow tan Guernsey cows was just as fascinating to her as possibly figuring out a way to catch a golden catfish without being stung by its whiskers. Also, she was older and more responsible. So, my city cousin continued up the lane, while I followed the golden prize as it swam down the shallow stream.

The stream, at the end of the lane, emptied into a canal, where the catfish could escape into deeper waters.

This was a time for a great decision. I ran back to the milk barn to get a coffee can to catch the catfish. Nothing else mattered now that I had decided to catch my golden prize.

For a short time I had been outside the immediate reach of my stepfather, but still under his observation; and when my city cousin continued alone on her way to fetch the cows my stepfather wasn't pleased.

As I entered the corral I heard, "Come here," from the man who was now my stepfather. I realized I'd have to pay for ignoring my cow fetching duty.

"Look up there. Your cousin is 'rounding-up' the cows and you're back here playing around. What's your excuse?"

Would he understand my excitement about seeing the fish? Probably not I thought. But I tried.

"I saw a fish . . . a golden fish in the irrigation ditch. I want to catch the fish before it gets into the canal."

"She (the city cousin) can get the cows," might have been added in a sarcastic tone.

My step dad, with love, could have said, "Let's go see this golden fish." But instead he said, "Your cousin isn't going to get those cows alone when I told you to show her how to get them. Forget the fish and stop playing around."

After a short staring contest between stepfather and me, he hit me on the side of the head over my left ear.

I heard a pop in my ear and started crying at the surprise and pain of the blow.

As nice a dream as the golden prize in the stream was, this confrontation, if it could be called a confrontation was a nightmare. This wasn't the price I had imagined I would have to pay for admission to the dream of catching the golden catfish waiting in the stream by the lane.

Would capturing the catfish make up for this nightmare? I thought as I shook my head and tried to clear my ear. When my ear cleared I heard my stepfather command, "You get up there and show your cousin how to get those cows down here!"

Very mindful of my recent misfortune, with my ear still ringing, I ran up the lane with a sideways glance at the stream to see how close the catfish was to the large canal.

Did the catfish know it had escaped being captured? I wondered. No, it just continued to swim and wriggle downstream in the small irrigation ditch. But it would get away if I didn't hurry along and help my cousin fetch the cows quickly.

Kathy had gotten between groups of cows and was trying to bring them together before herding them off the hill and into the lane. With my help we maneuvered the Guernsey and Holstein cows into one group and then past an ancient rusted out horse drawn hay rake (very spooky to the timid cows) partially hidden by tall weeds near the head of the lane.

As the milk cows, with full udders and dragging hooves, kicked up dust along the dusty lane, I waited impatiently to see whether or not the golden prize was still in the stream.

Had it gotten away? Was it already swimming safely in the large canal?

A wooden, homemade, swinging gate, anchored to sturdy deeply sunken, upright railroad ties, was just ahead of the lead cow that was swinging its head back and forth, chewing its cud, and swishing its tail at black flies. *Can't it walk faster,* I thought, anxious to accomplish the goal for which I had just suffered at the hands of my stepfather.

If the golden fish is there I can use the coffee can for measuring out feed for the milk cows, I thought, remembering all the mornings and nights I had measured out just so many cans of oats and just so many cans of ground grain for each cow as it stood quietly in its stall waiting its turn to be milked.

I'll use the coffee can to trap the fish and a wooden shingle to scoop it into the can, I day-dreamed and planned as I walked slowly behind the ambling herd of milk cows with my city cousin.

"Do you want to help me catch the catfish?" I enthusiastically questioned Kathy.

Fetching cows down from the hilly pasture had apparently been enough excitement for my city breed relative.

"No," she answered good-naturedly. "I want to help Aunt Margie in the garden." And that was the end of her involvement in a project she knew had caused her country cousin to cry; weren't there tear stains on his dusty cheeks, and wasn't there now a wet pattern on the front of his Levi jeans.

After the last cow had passed through the gate, and the gate was latched with a chain around the anchor post, I ran to the milk barn to get the red coffee can from the feed sack, and a shingle from the nearby wood pile.

When I arrived breathlessly back in the lane opposite the golden catfish, it was less than fifty feet from escaping the trickling stream and gaining its freedom in the irrigation canal.

Ducking between strands of sharp rusty barbed wire I spotted the golden dream wriggling as fast as it could in the shallow stream toward the large muddy canal.

Can I catch this fish? I thought excitedly, as I lowered the red coffee can behind the bright yellow catfish and scooped the fish into the can with the shingle. When I tipped the coffee can upright the catfish was trapped in the water at the bottom of the can.

Epilogue

I emptied the golden prize into a round water tank behind the milk barn. When my mother heard the complete story of how I had captured the catfish she made sure it could stay in the water tank as long as it lived. My stepfather was careful not to harm the fish, but regarded it evilly whenever he came near the water tank.

The catfish happily survived on mosses growing in the water at the bottom of the tank, and on unlucky insects that ended up on the water's surface at the top of the tank.

Occasionally a terrified cow would rear back in wide eyed surprise when the solitary catfish swam near the water's surface.

The nightmare encounter with my stepfather was the price of achieving my golden dream. The unpleasant encounter with my step dad hadn't been the first and it wouldn't be the last. The catfish lived for several months in the water tank as a reminder of the day.

My Fishing Hole

By Dennis Perry

As a boy,
I fished for rainbow trout,
in drainage ditches,
on hot summer days.
I caught my share,
of fish and mosquito bites.
When the fish
didn't bite
I closed my eyes,
to nap
on green banks.
My sun burned back,
bright red,
matched the sides
of the rainbow trout.

In my fishing hole,
culvert fed,
cool water flowed;
moments away
from farm and chores,
I got to play.
At the end of a field,
paradise revealed,
my fishing hole.

Bunky's Bad Luck Fishing Trip

In Bunky's Bad Luck Fishing Trip, *like my older cousin Butch, it was my turn to assume the role of protector of my younger brother Carl and younger cousin Bob.*

In my defense, both of these two characters were renegades when they were together.

The only thing left to do is to tell the story.

This fishing trip wasn't anything out of the ordinary. It was just us three young guys, dressed in blue jeans, stripped t-shirts and tennis shoes, taking our poles and bait to a drainage ditch running at the end of a neighbor's farm in southwestern Idaho.

As the oldest of the boys at twelve, in 1955, I was three years older, and for the only time in my life, two inches taller than both my brother Carl and my cousin Robert, who we called Bob. Because I was the oldest I was in-charge of the fishing trip.

Bob and I more closely resembled each other, both having brown hair. Carl had blonde hair and blue eyes while I had green eyes and Bob had brown eyes.

I had gone fishing in the same holes on the drainage ditch many times before. This was the only the second time I had taken both my brother and my cousin with me.

Fish, in particular, rainbow trout lived in the washed out holes just under and forward of the metal and concrete flumes that connected the drainage ditch when it passed under an earthen bridge to allow farmers access from one field to the next.

Regular fishermen never fished the drainage ditches, preferring the numerous and relatively close by fishing opportunities on the Snake River. They may also have been worried about the pesticide runoff from the farm fields, but didn't think that the drainage ditches finally emptied into larger canals that emptied into the Snake River at one point or another.

The most distant fishing hole we would be going to was only three quarters of a mile from our farm.

"Remember," my mother cautioned us, "don't go past Highway 30. It's off-limits, you understand. And be back in time to do your chores before dinner."

As the oldest, I was in-charge. Actually, between the three of us, back then, I was the most sensible and reliable. Carl and Bob always played together and generally ganged up against me when they wanted to do something their way.

A dusty weed lined road led away from the front of our farm house to the drainage ditch at the end of the south field.

We all happily scuffed our tennis shoes in the dust and kicked rocks which left dusty skid marks until they finally rolled and tumbled to a stop.

At the drainage ditch we ducked through barbed wire fences and hopped over single strand electric fences placed to keep cattle and sheep away from the drainage ditch.

Now we all talked and joked about our last fishing trip.

"This time we had better keep our t-shirts on if we decide to go swimming," I said.

On our last trip we had taken our shirts off at noon on a hot sunny day. Splashing and swimming in the drainage ditch we had gotten painfully sunburned; our backs turning a bright cooked lobster red.

I cautioned my two fishing companions, "Old man Williams doesn't want us on his property, so you guys don't cross over to his side of the drainage ditch. Stay on the Olsen's side of the ditch and we won't get in trouble this time."

"What's so good about his place that we can't walk over there?" was Bob's question.

"Hunters have spooked his cattle too many times and he thinks we'll do the same thing. Anyway it's no harder walking here than it would be on his side of the ditch."

"Yah, yah, okay," Bob said. "I really don't care where we walk. I just wanted to know the reason why, that's all."

"Well, I hope we have good luck at the first fishing hole. I caught my biggest trout there. And, if you guys don't jump into the hole after the first fifteen minutes I might catch another big one."

"You aren't our boss you know. We can do what we want. If we want to have a little fun you can't stop us," Bob said.

Aunt Jo Ann and uncle Earl expect me to be in-charge, so no swimming unless I say it's okay."

We walked along through clover, stinging nettles and Canadian thistles with their purple caps and broad prickly leaves. Monarch butterflies, in orange and black floated on the air, lighting on the blossoms in their paths.

A Mountain Blue bird, the state bird of Idaho, hopped from fence post to fence post along the ditch bank. It stayed just ahead of us on our way to the first fishing hole.

As we walked along we saw small fresh mounds of dirt that meant gophers were at work. Carl and Bob started chanting the old summer camp ditty-Greasy Grimy Gopher Guts and Bunky Too. They were referring to the traps I set to catch gophers.

Gophers were a threat to farmers because they could dig tunnels hundreds of feet long starting at the top of a field where irrigation water flowed into the tunnels and missed irrigating a big part of ground before emerging somewhere farther along in the field.

After catching the gophers I cut off their tails and took them to the County Ditch Company for a quarter a tail. I made movie money for weekends during the summer by trapping the gophers.

The box traps I normally used broke a gopher's ribs and suffocated it. But for smarter gophers I sometimes used a green wire trap called a 'gut trap'. Gut traps were somewhat like a large bear trap in principle only a lot smaller and with sharp tongs instead of jaws. When a gopher crawled across the gut trap it was sprung and ripped into the gopher's soft belly exposing its guts.

I didn't mind being teased because I had made a lot of money catching gophers and planned to go on making more money in the same way.

The first fishing hole didn't look any different from the rest of the holes we might try. It had a dirt bridge over a large corrugated metal flume. Water emptied into a deep hole in the ditch, dug out by the force of the water tumbling from the pipe. The depth of water in the ditch depended on runoff from the surrounding farms.

We picked comfortable spots on the ditch bank to sit and fish. We took worms out of a coffee can and baited our hooks.

With our lines in the water all that remained for us was the excitement of catching the first fish, and the boredom of waiting for fish that maybe weren't even biting.

Now Bob, who wasn't very patient, thought it would be more fun to look for odd shaped stones by the fishing hole. Shoving Carl into the fishing hole also seemed like a good idea. Once someone fell into the water the fish would be scared away and it would be time for a general swimming session.

Of the three of us, I was the most dedicated fisherman. I would try to keep my brother and cousin from fighting, if only to keep them from ruining my chances of catching a big one.

"Do you think we could find arrow heads here?" Bob asked.

"Are you kidding? Indians haven't lived here for more than one hundred years. And, besides this ground has been plowed and farmed for more than seventy-five years. If there were any arrow heads here someone would have found them a long time ago."

"Well, what do you think we could find here?"

"You might find some empty shot gun shells, or dried up water snake skins, or bird feathers; maybe a cow's horn or two, nothing very exciting. Why do you have to find anything? Why can't you just sit and watch your line?"

After twenty minutes passed, Bob started whining about going on to the next hole.

"You know we're not going to catch anything. If they aren't biting now they won't bite. Why don't we go on to the next hole and see if we can do better there?"

"We won't catch anything at the next hole. The next hole is on the upstream side of the big highway flume. The fish never stay on the upstream side; they swim through the pipe to where the water slows down on the other side, and you know we're not supposed to cross the highway," I added.

"Well, you know we won't catch any fish until we go there. And besides Carl and I are just about to go swimming here," Bob threatened, smiling. He finished by throwing a rock into the ditch to prove the fishing hole wasn't any good.

I resisted their pleas to go to the next hole for another half hour. Finally they jumped in the ditch just downstream from the fishing hole. As they got more impatient to do something else they waded and splashed closer and closer to where I had my line in the water.

"Okay, okay we'll go to the next hole, but we have to be very careful when we cross the highway.

Carl and Bob crawled out of the water and put their pants and shoes back on.

I reeled in my line and attached the hook to the eye nearest the reel. Bob and Carl grabbed their poles and the bait can, and the three of us started on our way.

I tried livening up the walk with a story, "Hey, did you guys hear about the giant sucker that hooked onto a kid on the Snake River and dragged him under until he drowned?"

"No way, you're making it up."

"I'm telling the truth. The kid's parents organized a search party and they found what was left of the body with a big sucker mark on his back."

Bob shock his head and said, "I heard the same kind of story but it was about some kids who were hooking giant catfish under river banks on the Mississippi River. One of the kids who had a hook for a hand hooked into a big one and before he could get the hook loose from his arm it pulled him under water. He couldn't get loose from the hook and he drowned. He lost the hand in a firecracker accident," Bob added at the end of the story.

"No man, I heard that one before and it's definitely just a story. The giant sucker thing really happened," I said as I climbed through a barbed wire fence separating one farmer's property from the next farm.

Carl and Bob followed him through the fence. They laughed and shoved each other as they caught up to me.

"It could have been a sturgeon. There are a lot of big sturgeons in the Snake River." Bob said.

"Yah, I've seen pictures of sturgeons long enough to hang over the end of a hay wagon.

But I've never heard of a sturgeon attacking a man or a boy," Carl added his two cents worth.

"Okay, okay. It was just a story anyway. I don't care if it was true or not."

We had arrived at the end of the farmer's property where we would have to decide whether or not to cross Highway 30.

"Well, are we going to cross the highway or not," Carl asked.

"That's the only way we're going to catch anything. So it's no use going all this way if we're not going to cross the highway," Bob added.

"I know we have to cross the highway I said, casting the deciding vote.

"We have to be really careful when we cross the road. We have to wait until there aren't any cars coming from either direction and then we run across. When we get across please don't go wading in this hole. I'd like to catch at least one trout before we go home."

One by one we climbed up and over the sheep proof wire fence that separated the farm from the highway. When we were down and by the side of the black topped asphalt highway Carl and Bob waited for me to give them the signal to cross the road.

Cars whizzed by at 50 and 60 miles per hour on the way back and forth between Boise and Nampa. The drivers may have glanced at us beside the road but few of them slowed down at all.

When a gap in the speeding cars and trucks appeared, I led the way across the highway, running to the barbed wire fence separating the highway from the next farm. We ducked through it and were then ready to settle down and fish in the new hole.

I took my hook loose and put a fresh worm on it. Carl and Bob weren't as interested in fishing but they also baited their hooks and dropped lines in the water. Cattails and Cow Lilies crowded the water beneath the concrete flume. Red Wing Blackbirds flew from one Cattail to another making bird sounds. A clear blue sky framed the yellow sun as it warmed the dusty earthen ditch banks.

It didn't take long for Carl and Bob to decide that they had fished enough for the day.

"It's too hot here. If we can't go swimming we need something to drink," Bob said.

"Yah, we could walk up to the Ten Mile Store and buy some RC's and candy bars," Carl said.

Carl and Bob nodded at each other and Carl said, "We'll find empty beer and pop bottles along the highway and collect the deposits on them when we get to the store."

"That's a good plan, but I don't think you should go. We're already in trouble for crossing the highway."

"Come on, we'll be right back and we'll get you something while we're there," Carl promised me.

I put my hand in my jeans pocket and brought out two nickels.

"Get me a Baby Ruth," I told Carl.

I didn't want them to go, but I also knew that if they went to the store they wouldn't be wading in the drainage ditch and ruining my chances for catching a big trout.

The boys ducked through the barbed wire fence and were on their way.

Soon after the boys left I felt a nibble on my hook. I let the nibbling continue, and then suddenly jerked the pole so the hook would set in the fishes' mouth. When I felt the fish wriggling on the end of my line I started reeling in and then lifted the line out of the water. At the end of my line I saw a small Minnow. We called the Minnows Shiners because of the colorful stripes on their sides. The Shiner flopped on the ditch bank until I took the bloody hook out of its mouth and threw it back into the water.

The thought crossed my mind that this small fish wasn't much, but it proved there were fish in the hole. Now if my brother and cousin would stay away long enough I might have a chance to catch something bigger.

While I fished and dozed under the warm sun by the fishing hole I thought of Carl and Bob walking the three miles to the small grocery store where they would buy sodas and candy bars with the deposit money from the pop bottles and beer bottles they collected on the way to the store.

Later, Carl told me that on the way to the store he and Bob stayed well away from the road walking in the grassy barrow pit. The bottles they were looking for were in the grass and weeds.

When they had all the bottles they could carry they walked closer to the road out of the weeds that planted hitchhikers and burrs in their socks and pant cuffs.

"It's not that much farther," Carl said, pointing at the group of buildings in the distance.

The Perry family shopped at the 10 Mile Grocery Store when they didn't want to drive to Meridan to the east or Nampa to the west of their farm. The owners, Sam and Ellen Cooper knew all the local farm people. In addition to the small grocery store and gas station, they also ran a bar and grill where families were welcome.

When Carl and Bob entered the grocery store with their arms full of pop bottles and beer bottles, Ellen Cooper wanted to know where the boys' parents were.

Carl looked at Bob. Neither of them had thought that they would have to have a story about why they were at the grocery store without their parents.

Just then Mrs. Cooper got called into the bar and her husband came into the store from pumping gas.

"What can I do for you two?" he asked the boys.

"We want to turn these bottles in for the deposit so we can buy some sodas," Bob was quick to explain.

"Yah," Carl added, "we want some candy bars too."

"Well, let's see how much you've got here Sam Cooper said, and he counted out the dimes and nickels they had coming.

"What will you boys have?" Sam asked again after giving the boys their money.

Carl bought an RC soda and three candy bars, two Three Musketeers and a Baby Ruth. Baby Ruth was my favorite.

Bob bought an orange Fanta and two candy bars.

As soon as they had paid their money the two boys grabbed their sodas and candy bars and hurried out the door before Mrs. Cooper came back and finished asking about their parents.

"I thought we were in trouble," Bob said when they were away from the store.

"Yah, she probably would've called my mother and she would've come and got us. She wouldn't have been happy about it either."

"Let's wait till we get back to the ditch before we drink our sodas. Bunky won't have one, but it's his fault for not coming along."

"Yah, okay," Bob said.

Back at the store Ellen asked Sam if he had found out what those Perry boys were doing at the store alone.

"Gee, I didn't think anything about it," he replied. "We're not responsible for everyone who comes in here you know."

Ellen heaved a sigh and said she hoped they would be okay.

At the drainage ditch I hadn't had another bite since I caught the Minnow and tossed it back in the fishing hole.

I could have gone with Carl and Bob, I thought. *I wonder when they will get back. I'll bet they're still goofing off at the store.*

I decided to wait a little while longer and then start back home without them. It didn't occur to me to walk towards the store to see if I could find them.

It will be their faults if they got in trouble. I told them it wasn't right to go to the store.

After a little while I reeled in my line and took the worm off of the hook. I fastened the hook onto the eye nearest the reel, picked up the bait can, put my fishing pole over my shoulder and started walking home.

Instead of climbing over fences and stumbling along the weedy ditch bank, I decided to take the longer, but easier way home, walking by the side of Highway 30 until I got to the gravel road that led to our farm about a mile and a half away.

Walking along the dusty dirt and gravel road I had a bad feeling about leaving Carl and Bob.

I should have stayed with them. Just as I was thinking this thought I heard the wail of a siren coming from Nampa. I continued walking until I reached home. No one was there. I knew something very bad had happened. I put my fishing rod and reel in the garage and sat down on the front porch, waiting for someone to come home. I hadn't caught any fish, at least, no fish that would have made the trip worthwhile. Also, I thought, *Carl and Bob were still somewhere between the store and home.*

Epilogue

Back on Highway 30, on the way back to the fishing hole from the store, Bob had seen a bit of shining metal across the highway. He had started to cross the road to inspect the shiny piece, and the moment he stepped onto the pavement from the barrow pit a car appeared out of nowhere, the car door handle had grazed his forehead as he tried to duck back out of the way.

The car's driver had stopped immediately and reversed to where Bob was laying in the barrow pit. Once he saw Bob was alive but bleeding badly, he drove to a nearby farm house and called for an ambulance.

The ambulance, dispatched from Nampa, raced to the scene of the accident and its siren was the wailing noise I'd heard.

At the hospital, doctors examined Bob and said he had a concussion and needed 70 stitches to his forehead, but they thought he would be okay.

My mother, Margie, stepfather, Everett, and my aunt Jo Ann and uncle Earl all wanted to know why we had crossed Highway 30. And why had I let Carl and Bob go to the store without going with them.

I admitted I didn't have any excuse for what they had done and I was very sorry for what had happened.

Cousin Bob recovered from the accident and later survived a tour of duty in Vietnam where he was promoted to sergeant. Carl also went to Vietnam, served in the Navy Sea Bees, and was promoted to Petty Officer 2nd class.

I joined the Navy after graduating from High School and served two of my four years in the service aboard an aircraft carrier off of the coast of Vietnam. I held the rank of Petty Officer 3rd class at the end of my service. I got back to the states just in time to start college as a freshman with Robert.

This poem is a prelude to the following story. It illustrates an idealized walk home without regard to property or right aways.

The Shortcut Home

Orchard Ridge* was
where I climbed
plumb trees and apple trees
after school.
An irrigation ditch
flowed-enclosed
by lush greenery,
dividing
farmers' fields.
Fast running water
led me home,
through new mown hay;
a place to play,
where green grasses grew.
Pastures and ponds
were mine to enjoy-
the race of boy.
Miles from home,
my shortcut,
a nature walk, was
filled with true wonders
of the natural world.

I followed muddy waters
to a mossy pond,
a mirror to the sun.
The pond overflowed,
green shouldered,
streaming through

a snug meadow.
Blackbirds called
from birds' nests
in cottonwood trees,
by the stream.
Cattails and pussy willows
Mimicked, in name, the animal world
of field mice and frogs fleeing
their sky soaring enemy-
the barn owl.

A gray paper wasps' nest,
better avoided hung,
in a wild rose tree.
And me, the enemy
of our neighbors
Blackberry bushes;

I raided like a pirate.
My juice stained chin-
a black beard.
All this was my world.
A nature walk,
my shortcut home
after school.

* Orchard Ridge was the one room school house where I
attended first and second grades.

Bunky at
the Weir Gate

While working as a librarian in Chicago, Illinois, I took my vacations visiting several Mississippian Native American sites. One thing all of these sites had in common was a great peacefulness.

The sites may not have been peaceful while they were occupied by the early Native Americans; but I'm absolutely sure the sites were originally chosen for their calmness and tranquility.

The small vale by Perisal's Pond, described in Bunky at the Weir Gate *had the same peacefulness as the sites I visited during my vacations.*

Just walking through such a place was like being in a church or even a cathedral built by nature.

As a child growing up, it was my privilege to spend time in that small retreat away from the world outside it.

At that time I was always aware that I was a trespasser. The glen belonged to our neighbor. As a child, and later as a teenager, I only wanted to experience nature there, not to change it in any way.

I was lucky to have had access to Perisal's Pond and the glen during my growing up years. Then a dispute between adults over water rights ended my visits to the pond and the vale.

I walked along the edge of a drying hay field that needed irrigation. It was early morning on a Saturday. No school today-only farm chores.

At fourteen years old I was on my way to release water into our irrigation ditches from the county water canal. Access to the county water supply first passed through the Perisal farm where Mr. Perisal had illegally stopped up county water by building a holding pond to water his cattle and raise catfish. He also used the pond for duck hunting in the fall.

The Perisals were once good friends with the Perrys until they started arguing over the illegal damming of county water. Now, although the county water right of way for the Perry farm passed through Perisal's lower meadow he considered it trespassing for anyone crossing his meadow to get to the irrigation weir that released water from his pond into a series of ditches that irrigated the upper fields of the Perry farm.

As I tromped along in my black rubber irrigation boots I was thinking more about the green frogs that leaped into the canal from the tall weeds than about the argument between the Perisals and the Perrys. When I was younger I had led my brothers Carl and Buddy on frog catching expeditions many times. We didn't keep the frogs after we caught them. The joy of catching the green amphibians was a basic instinct for small boys who in earlier times would have become hunter gatherers.

I remembered the small leopard frogs, with yellow spots outlined by black circles on dark green skin, as feeling somewhat cold from being in the water; but they definitely weren't slimy like some people thought. Also, the harmless garter snakes we had handled and sometimes killed out of ignorance weren't slimy either. But somehow it had always seemed right to chuck a rock at something wriggling along silently in the grassy fields.

As my mind drifted away from thinking about frogs and snakes, I turned my thoughts to the last year in Junior High. I had been disappointed when I couldn't get algebra like the smart kids in Mr. Johns' class. (I would need algebra to take college classes in the natural sciences.) Mr. Johns had separated his classes into three levels-those who always had their assignments done and wanted extra credit, those who understood what they were doing and more or less kept up in class, and the third group of students, my group, the kids who didn't know what was going on and who couldn't keep up.

Mr. Johns had no pity on this group and gave them little of his time. I and the rest of the group held back the advanced group in the class because we took up precious time Mr. Johns could be giving to the kids who were more on his level and not quite so boring to work with.

After struggling to keep up I finally gave up and resigned myself to a D in algebra. I hoped I could make up for low grades in algebra by doing well in English.

I didn't have to struggle in English class. I was a natural born reader. I loved books and I was also a student of human nature; and that allowed me to more easily understand what I read concerning human behavior. More than once teachers had sent me to sit at the back of the class because I had asked embarrassing questions and stared a little too hard at the teacher.

If I remembered Mr. Johns for a bad reason, I remember my seventh grade social studies teacher as a sensitive person who required all of us in her classes to keep scrap books of lynching in the south. The year was 1956 and our scrap books had many entries before the school year was done.

At this same time I started going to the Saturday afternoon movies alone. At the concession counter there were red and black licorice pieces. It was our habit to call these pieces nigger babies and Indian babies. This poor behavior was of the times. But even in the fifties, in a small town thousands of miles from the racism happening elsewhere, a local teacher called the problem to the attention of her seventh graders. I'm sure we had our own version of racism directed against the Mexicans who hoed the beet fields and harvested whatever crops that needed harvesting.

I wish I had my scrap book to remind of the brave and sensitive social studies teacher.

It was a bright sunny day as I continued along the lower fields of our farm. The wheat field on my left hand side needed water. I could see the ground had dried up and started to crack where the irrigation furrows connected to the larger irrigation ditches. After I opened the weir gate and released water into the lead irrigation ditches, the water would soak into the ground and turn it muddy brown.

Although Mr. Perisal and my stepfather no longer considered themselves friends it didn't occur to me there might be a problem raising the weir gate. If truth be told, I had caused my share of friction between the two families by raiding the blackberry bushes Mr. Perisal had planted along the small lead irrigation ditch running from Perisal's Pond to the lower fields of the Perry farm. Now my brothers and I were under strict orders not to visit the Perisal property, except to raise or lower the weir gate.

My thoughts again drifted to school when I saw a large grasshopper spring away from the ditch bank into the dry wheat field. Mr. Haygood, a biology teacher, and one of my favorite teachers had given a class assignment to bring in insect collections. Each collection would have thirty insects in a cigar box lined with cotton batting from a first aid kit.

I had walked these same ditch banks collecting unusual insects to fill my cigar box. Each insect I trapped was properly anesthetized in a ball fruit jar with a drop of alcohol on a cotton swab dropped into the jar. Then the unlucky insect was mounted on a sewing needle pushed through the insect's thorax and stuck into the bottom of the cigar box.

My collection included the usual ladybugs, grasshoppers and water skippers, or water striders. I included a beautiful purple and blue dragonfly and a huge water beetle, not to be confused with a giant water bug, whose bite could be very painful I had discovered.

Of course every farm kid in the school district had most of the same bugs in their cigar boxes, but Mr. Haygood made a big deal out of displaying all the collections in his classroom and made a lot of points with his students.

My cigar box was donated by the Ten Mile Store and Gas Station where my parents bought groceries when they didn't want to drive to Nampa or Meridian. Also, the Ten Mile Store gave our family a charge account that wasn't possible at the Safeway store in town.

The fence line between the Perisal property and the Perry farm was only steps ahead of me. I would cross the fence by holding up one of the barbed wire strands and ducking under it. This particular section of fencing wasn't electrified because no cattle were being kept on either side of the fence.

When I straightened up on the other side of the fence Strang's Sand and Gravel pit was on my left hand. Two summers earlier, on a weekend, four teenage boys were using the sand chutes where trucks were loaded as a thrill ride; sliding down the sand hills and dropping through the chute to the empty loading area below. One of the boys had started through the chute, but he had hooked his leg over an iron bar for catching trash in the center of the chute and stopped right there. He couldn't get out and his friends couldn't pull him out or keep the sand from pouring down the hill and pressing against his chest.

With each minute that went by the boy was having a more difficult time breathing.

Just at this time I was walking along the edge of the sand pit on my way home from a fishing trip. I saw the three boys atop the hill frantically trying to dig their friend out of the sand chute and went closer to find out what was happening.

One of the boys told me about the boy stuck in the sand chute and said, "Go to your house and tell your father a boy is stuck in a sand chute, and to bring the biggest shovel he has to help dig him out."

I walked and ran home, where I told my stepfather what the boy at the sand pit had said. My stepfather knew there was a big problem and called the Nampa fire department out on an emergency run. Then he drove to the closed gate at the sand pit and hurried to the sand chute where the sand continued to pour down and pack in tightly, grain by grain, against the trapped boy's chest. The boy could hardly talk and his eyes were starting to become blood shot.

Everett Perry used his scoop shovel as best he could to keep the mountain of sand from settling in waves against the trapped boy, but he couldn't stop it all.

After ten minutes the fire department crew arrived and the fire fighters ran up the sand hill to see what they could do to rescue the trapped and suffocating boy.

The fire truck was equipped with axes and poles but not shovels, so they all took turns using my stepfather's scoop shovel to try and clear away the sand pressing in against the boy's chest. Some of the firefighters went into the chute to loosen the iron bar that had trapped the boy but they couldn't get to it because of the sand pushed up tightly around the boy's thighs.

The men back on the sand hill decided to hose down the sand above the chute to stop it from sliding downward. This maneuver only caused the sand to be heavier as it packed in more solidly against the trapped boy.

By this time the boy was hardly breathing so the fire fighters got a respirator off the fire engine and adjusted it over the boy's mouth. Even with the respirator the boy couldn't take a breath because his chest had been compressed by the sand.

This event had a sad ending when the trapped boy suffocated in front of the fire fighters, his three friends, me and my stepfather.

Everyone had done what they could to rescue the boy but it hadn't worked.

The boys had been trespassing in a dangerous area and one of them had died because of it.

The day of the boy's death was otherwise memorable for me because an ant had bitten me on the lower lip while I watched the men trying to rescue the boy, and my lip had swollen up twice normal size.

Just ahead I could see the peaceful meadow below Perisal's Pond. On my way home from first and second grade when I was still allowed to take the shortcut home, I had stopped many times in this meadow to enjoy the solitude and watch nature.

Migrating ducks and geese used the pond to raise their ducklings and goslings during the summer months. Wasps built their paper nests in the wild rose bushes. The willows and cottonwood trees shaded the meadow along the small stream that ran through it.

In the fall, when the county cut the water supply, the stream was reduced to many muddy puddles where my brothers, cousins and I caught the trapped minnows and suckers to feed the barn cats gathered around our dairy barn.

All of this activity took place on property belonging to the Perisals. Up until the dispute about the irrigation water no one had objected to these activities. Now the Perisals didn't want any of the Perry family on their property for any reason whatsoever.

On this particular day I was thinking about everything and anything except the fact I was trespassing on the Perisals' farm.

I walked along the shallow stream in the meadow through the wild rose bushes with the red and pink blossoms, approaching the wheeled weir gate that raised and lowered a metal plate to allow water to escape Perisal Pond and flow into the irrigation ditch running across Perisal's property to our farm.

The weir gate sat below a raised earth and rock dam. As I neared the weir I couldn't see over the top of the dam. I was concentrating on the metal wheel of the gate I would soon be turning to release water from Perisal's Pond.

After I finished opening the gate I thought I would take a little time and look around the pond. I wouldn't be playing like I did in grade school. I would be observing nature like I had learned to do in biology class.

At the moment I put my hands on the metal wheel, two heads wearing caps appeared over the edge of the dam.

Mr. Perisal and his son Darryl came over the top of the dam. Darryl Perisal was four years older than me and had assumed all the importance of the late teen years. He helped his father farm their property just as I helped my stepfather on the Perry farm. But, unlike me he would become a farmer in his own right.

When the Perisals were standing at the top of the dam I could see Mr. Perisal had a shotgun in his hands. My own hands stopped turning the weir gate. I stared at the Perisals as they continued to walk up the small knoll built up around the weir gate and water discharge pipe.

I was squatting on my heels like a Native American to turn the wheel, and as the Perisals came closer I had to tip back farther on my heels to keep them fully in view.

Mr. Perisal gestured toward me with the shotgun. The twelve gauge shotgun was now pointed threateningly at me.

"What do you think you're doing?" he asked me.

"I'm supposed to open the weir gate ten turns."

"The gate is on our property and you can't take water from the pond without our permission. You have to tell Everett that." Mr. Perisal told me still pointing the shotgun purposely in my direction.

I sort've knew a problem existed between the two families since my brothers and I had been forbidden from playing on the Perisal farm by our parents. In this situation I began to sense there was a bigger problem involving the water dammed up in Perisal's Pond. Who did the water belong to? Wasn't it a part of the county water delivery system? Anyway I couldn't return home and tell my stepfather I hadn't been allowed to open the weir gate.

I looked up at Mr. Perisal and said, "I'd rather you shoot me now than go home and tell Everett I didn't open the weir gate."

Then I tightened my grip on the metal wheel and continued to turn it until I had finished ten full turns.

Apparently I had spoken with enough conviction in my eyes and voice to convince Mr. Perisal what I had said was true.

When I stood up and turned away from Mr. Perisal and his son Darryl and started walking back along the irrigation ditch, now filling with water, towards our farm I realized I wouldn't be able to enjoy the peaceful meadow this time. I continued walking sadly to the fence that separated the two farms.

Epilogue

For the next two years the Perisal family sued the Perry family over access to the irrigation ditch running across the Perisal's farm. During this time Perisal's Pond was off limits to me.

The Perisals didn't win in court. The irrigation ditches in Canyon County had been established since my grandfather Perry rode the ditch banks as a ditch riding detective. He had carried a revolver while he toured the county ditches on horse back. Water disputes could arise over a weir gate being secretly opened at night and closed the next morning. Farmers might be best of friends one day and bitter enemies the next.

Even after the court determined Everett Perry had the right to maintain and use the irrigation ditch crossing the Perisal's property, Perisal's Pond remained off-limits.

If ever there was an Eden in Canyon County, I had been driven out of it, if not by God, then at least by man.

IDAHO
MEMORIES-POEMS

Idaho Memories

By Dennis Perry

I haven't forgotten Idaho,*
after many years
away from the farms
and open skies,
over open fields.

I remember how Idaho feels:
The Tetons in pine-tree blouses,
the foothills in sagebrush skirts,
waiting to be farmed
by industrious Mormons,
or some other flatlanders.

*Written after living away from Idaho for 24 years.

Big Blue Sky

By Dennis Perry

The big blue sky is heavy,
weighing down the land.
Big blue sky rubs off
on the mountains,
and drops heavily
in the mountain
streams.

River Music

By Dennis Perry

Shining wet river rocks,
In a wet river bed-
a nature laid,
rocky player piano roll;
where river water notes
are played,
and bubbling water music
is made.

Brothers

By Dennis Perry

A grassy pasture, green
from the summer sun.
A perfect place to run.
or lay and lean
on elbows bare.

Two brothers under the blue sky,
watching the clouds blow by,
enjoying the summer fare.
Chewing on grass stems.

Red Rover, Red Rover

By Dennis Perry

The children went out to play,
they couldn't stay in school all day,
listening to stories of ancient war
between the Greeks and Trojans, what a bore.

On school grounds they divided on the green lawn-
one group as followers of the Greek Agamemnon,
the other followed Paris, of Helen's beauty singing.
They would settle this dispute before the next bell rang.

The followers of Agamemnon and Ulysses ran hence,
across the playground up against the boundary fence.
The Trojans fell together, touching the sturdy stone wall
of the country school hall.

"Red Rover, Red Rover, send your best right over."
"Red Rover, Red Rover, we're sending Curtis right over.
The Paris crowd joined hands, making a human net.
They would capture Curtis, they were set.

Curtis ran across the field like Achilles after Hector.
He charged into their line, looking for the weakest vector.
First one side, then the other showed its mettle;
until the school bell rang, ending the battle.

From Homer the poet, to Homer the painter,
comes expressions of great deeds and banter,
in prose and pictures, on the fields of play
children will have their warriors' day.

On The Way Home

(A second grader's odyssey) By Dennis Perry

I took a long time
walking home
after school.
I was fascinated
by the barrow,
by the gravel,
by the road.

Green pastures lazed
under a blue sky.
A cottonwood tree
called to me, "Come
swing on my branches.
Don't hurry home,
swing high, to the sky.
Listen to my birds sing."

There was no candy store
nearby, so I stopped
and played
on the way home.

The Dead Boy
and the Sand Pit

By Dennis Perry

Ancient sand dunes-
weed scabbed;
soft breezes sooth you
where men and machines
have scratched you bare.

Four merry boys strayed
beyond your grass,
onto sandy hills,
past no trespass.

They found dangerous play
riding your sandy tide-
a thrill filled ride.
But the State Fair was over,
death waited past the clover.

There was no mention of graves
as the four sailed sandy waves.
Sliding through a sandy trap,
no rider heard one hand clap.

Three sad boys left a future farm hand
in your quick sand.

A Fall Collection

By Dennis Perry

Clear fields,
bring in,
stack up,
heap over.
Burn clean.
Bleed and render.
Set by,
mend,
bundle up,
wear shoes.

Sweat

By Dennis Perry

Sling hay bales high
above your head.
Hay leaves and sweat,
the worst enemies
you've ever met.

Under a hot sun
walking many miles,
always itching,
quit your bitching.

Hear the wagon creaking
under hay bales peaking,
toward an Aztec sun.
After a long day
you'll be too tired
to play.

Reaching for the Stars

By Dennis Perry

I stand tall, hands high,
under the night sky.
leaving empty star sockets,
I fill my pockets
with bright tokens,
and a destination opens
of hope and grace,
my secret place.

Pretty Girl

By Dennis Perry

Pretty girl *
if I had your looks
I wouldn't be
buried in books.
With that face
aren't you
out of place?
Who's to blame,
for appearances sake
if you're not ashamed.

*My favorite librarian

Old Car

By Dennis Perry

You've driven many miles,
given me lots of smiles.
Old car,
old paint,
you're engine isn't much,
but you haven't lost your touch.
With gas
in your tank,
for the long ride
you've got your pride.
You and me
we're the same.

Hitchhiking

By Dennis Perry

He had a thumb
like a stop sign.
Drivers stopped every time
his feet hit the road.
As a passenger
he kept conversation
to a minimum.
Front seat or rear
he made it clear he was just a passenger.
The open road
flew by for free.
The experience became everything;
meeting good
and not so good people.
Who said hitchhikers
are dangerous?
There are plenty
of dangerous drivers
out there.

Donut Man

By Dennis Perry

Donut man you've been there.
I know you cared,
for a hungry bum,
on the run.

Donuts, chocolate covered,
given to one who hovered
at your shop-
a desperate stop.
I haven't forgotten.

Shadows

By Dennis Perry

Water barer-
thirty years later
your shadow
fills my dreams.
Shadow caster,
your brown eyes,
and smile-
your reds and yellows
and greens,
become a black and white
silent movie.
Exaggerated at night,
by lantern light,
your tall shadow
moves weary,
but graceful
on the village wall
in my mind.

Buy My Book

By Dennis Perry

Everyone who's written
one, a book, I mean,
knows what I'm talking about,
Buy my book.

Homer. Dickens and Twain
to name a few,
had stories to spew.
Buy my book.

Ezra Pound, T.S. Eliot
and Walt Whitman
were in the trade.
From their words
poems were made.
Buy my book.

When I started writing
my fingers were longer
then,
and my pencils too.
Buy my book.

The words wore me down,
caused a frown,
Buy my book.

Words, sentences, paragraphs,
and chapters to spin.
Buy my book.

Copyrights, movie rights,
protect my words on paper,
and in electronic media.
I've got my rights.
Buy my book.

Just the same,
I won't die
if you don't
Buy my book.